Inside Out and Back Again
Novel Unit

A collection of teacher resources for the novel *Inside Out and Back Again* by Thanhha Lai

Heather C. Flor

TABLE OF CONTENTS

A NOTE ON THESE RESOURCES

These activities have been prepared with ease of the teacher in mind. Every class varies, and teachers will want to add their own projects and assignments as needed. However, the assignments in this book provide plenty of opportunities for students to engage with the text. Features of note include:

- Multiple choice questions split by part of the book so that they may be given as individual quizzes or compiled for a unit test.
- Essay rubrics with descriptions entered, but no point values, so that the instructor may customize these forms to fit his or her needs.
- Definitions of key literary terms and poetic devices within reading questions to aide students as they apply knowledge to answer questions.

Unless otherwise noted, all short quotations in this book are from:
   Lai, Thanhha. *Inside out & Back Again*. New York: Harper, 2013. Print.

Common Core English Language Arts Standards

STANDARD	ACTIVITIES IN THIS UNIT
CCSS.ELA-LITERACY.CCRA.R.1 Read closely to determine what the text says explicitly and to make logical inferences from it; cite specific textual evidence when writing or speaking to support conclusions drawn from the text.	Reading comprehension and analysis questions Essay questions
CCSS.ELA-LITERACY.CCRA.R.2 Determine central ideas or themes of a text and analyze their development; summarize the key supporting details and ideas.	Essay questions
CCSS.ELA-LITERACY.CCRA.R.3 Analyze how and why individuals, events, or ideas develop and interact over the course of a text.	Reading comprehension and analysis questions Essay questions
CCSS.ELA-LITERACY.CCRA.R.4 Interpret words and phrases as they are used in a text, including determining technical, connotative, and figurative meanings, and analyze how specific word choices shape meaning or tone.	Reading comprehension and analysis questions
CCSS.ELA-LITERACY.CCRA.R.5 Analyze the structure of texts, including how specific sentences, paragraphs, and larger portions of the text (e.g., a section, chapter, scene, or stanza) relate to each other and the whole.	Reading comprehension and analysis questions Essay questions
CCSS.ELA-LITERACY.CCRA.R.7 Integrate and evaluate content presented in diverse media and formats, including visually and quantitatively, as well as in words.	Anticipation guide
CCSS.ELA-LITERACY.CCRA.R.10 Read and comprehend complex literary and informational texts independently and proficiently.	Reading comprehension and analysis questions Comprehension check multiple choice questions

CCSS.ELA-LITERACY.CCRA.W.1 Write arguments to support claims in an analysis of substantive topics or texts using valid reasoning and relevant and sufficient evidence.	Essay questions
CCSS.ELA-LITERACY.CCRA.W.4 Produce clear and coherent writing in which the development, organization, and style are appropriate to task, purpose, and audience.	Essay questions
CCSS.ELA-LITERACY.CCRA.W.5 Develop and strengthen writing as needed by planning, revising, editing, rewriting, or trying a new approach.	Essay questions
CCSS.ELA-LITERACY.CCRA.L.1 Demonstrate command of the conventions of standard English grammar and usage when writing or speaking.	Essay questions
CCSS.ELA-LITERACY.CCRA.L.2 Demonstrate command of the conventions of standard English capitalization, punctuation, and spelling when writing.	Essay questions
CCSS.ELA-LITERACY.CCRA.L.5 Demonstrate understanding of figurative language, word relationships, and nuances in word meanings.	Reading comprehension and analysis questions

ANTICIPATION GUIDE

Agree or Disagree?

Instructions: Read each of the following statements. Then, indicate whether you agree, somewhat agree, somewhat disagree, or disagree with each statement by writing your answer on the line.

> **A = agree**
> **SA = somewhat agree**
> **SD = somewhat disagree**
> **D = disagree**

1. _____ When in danger, running away to safety is the best option.

2. _____ Happy moments and memories cannot exist in the same place and time as bombings and war.

3. _____ Making decisions is easy if you examine all of the facts.

4. _____ Being a new student at school is exciting.

5. _____ The most difficult part of learning a new language is understanding all of the rules of grammar.

6. _____ Fulfilling your own desires and goals in life is more important than pleasing your parents.

7. _____ A mother will always put the needs of her children first.

8. _____ Grief is easier to bear if it is shared.

9. _____ The history and heritage of one's country defines the person.

10. _____ People cannot have a fresh start until they have let go of their past.

Name _____

ANTICIPATION GUIDE

Fɪʀsᴛ Lᴏᴏᴋ ᴀᴛ ᴛʜᴇ Bᴏᴏᴋ

1. Look at the cover of the book. What awards and honors has the book received?

   _____

   _____

2. What do you notice first about the artwork and design on the cover? _____

   _____

   _____

3. Based on the cover, what do you think the book will be about? _____

   _____

   _____

4. Read the plot preview and critical reviews of the book. Based on these, list one reason

   why you might find the book interesting. _____

   _____

   _____

Read the poem "Early Monsoon" at the start of the book.

5. What is a monsoon? _____

6. What is the noise described in the poem? _____

   _____

7. What is the date of the poem? _____

8. To whom is the book dedicated? _____

9. What is a refugee? _____

   _____

Inside Out and Back Again
Thanhha Lai

Name _____

ANTICIPATION GUIDE

QUICK BACKGROUND INFORMATION: THE VIETNAM WAR

- Vietnam is a small country in Southeast Asia. It is a bit larger than New Mexico.
- On September 2, 1945, Vietnam gained independence from France.
- An international conference in Geneva on November 1, 1955 split Vietnam into a communist North and a noncommunist South.
- The start of United States involvement in the Vietnam War is not definitive. During the late 1950s and early 1960s, United States support of South Vietnam increased.
- During the Vietnam War, the United States supported noncommunist South Vietnam against communist North Vietnam and their allies in the South, the Viet Cong.
- The United States withdrew combat forces from Vietnam in 1973.
- On April 30, 1975, North Vietnam gained control of Saigon, the capital of South Vietnam, ending the war and reunifying Vietnam under communist rule.
- Saigon is now called Ho Chi Minh City, and it is the most populous city in Vietnam.
- Over 3 million people, including 58,000 Americans, were killed in the Vietnam War.

"Battlefield: Vietnam." *PBS*. PBS. Web. 8 Mar. 2015. <http://www.pbs.org/battlefieldvietnam/timeline/>.

Carland, Dr. John. "Information Paper: When Did the Vietnam War Start for the United States?" *Vietnam War 50th*. Office of the Secretary of Defense, 17 June 2012. Web. 8 Mar. 2015. <http://www.vietnamwar50th.com/assets/1/7/Info_paper_Vietnam_War_and_US_Start_Date.pdf>.

"Vietnam." *Central Intelligence Agency*. Central Intelligence Agency, 3 Apr. 2013. Web. 5 Mar. 2015. <https://www.cia.gov/library/publications/cia-maps-publications/Vietnam.html>.

"Vietnam War." *History.com*. A&E Television Networks, 1 Jan. 2015. Web. 8 Mar. 2015. <http://www.history.com/topics/vietnam-war>.

"The World Factbook: Vietnam." *Central Intelligence Agency*. Central Intelligence Agency, 30 June 2014. Web. 8 Mar. 2015. <https://www.cia.gov/library/publications/the-world-factbook/geos/vm.html>.

Name _____

READING COMPREHENSION AND ANALYSIS QUESTIONS

Part I: Saigon

1. What is the year for the **setting** of the story? _____

2. What is Tết and how is it celebrated? _____

   _____

   _____

3. How old is the **narrator**? _____

4. What is the Teller of Fate's prediction for Hà's family? What do you think this means for

   the family? _____

   _____

   _____

5. Fill in the following chart for the characters in Hà's family:

Character	Descriptive Details
	Ten years old; named for the Golden River; loves her papaya tree
Mother	
Quang	
	Eighteen years old; idolizes Bruce Lee
Khôi	

6. A **symbol** is something used to represent another thing, person, or idea. Explain what papayas and the papaya tree symbolize in this novel. _____

_____

_____

_____

7. Who is TiTi? Where does she go? _____

_____

_____

8. What has happened to Hà's father? How does the family deal with his absence?

_____

_____

_____

9. What does Hà do when her mother sends her to the market to shop for the family?

_____

_____

_____

10. A **simile** is a comparison between two things using the words "like" or "as." Find an example of a simile in "Two More Papayas." _____

_____

11. Why are some words written in italics in this text? _____

_____

12. In the poems "Current News" and "TV News" Hà hears that what group is coming closer to Saigon? As these people come closer, how is Hà's family and community impacted?

_____

_____

13. How did Hà's mother become separated from her father and family in the North?

_____

_____

_____

14. In "A Day Downtown" Hà and her mother go to a ceremony for military wives. What comment does the President make to the crowd? What is Mother's response to the speech? _____

_____

_____

_____

15. Identify one **simile** in "Twisting Twisting." What does the simile show the reader about Mother? _____

_____

_____

16. What does Hà do to Tram? Why does she do it? _____

_____

_____

17. "Promises" is a poem about papayas on Hà's tree, which are **symbolic** of Hà. It says that the papayas "cling to the trunk" and they are "Still green / but promising." How can these lines be applied to Hà as well? _____

_____

_____

_____

18. Who is Uncle Sớn and what does he find for Hà's family? _____

_____

_____

_____

19. Mother asks for the sons' opinions about leaving VIetnam in "Should We?" Why is Vũ's answer different from his brothers'? _____

_____

_____

20. **Repetition** is the use of a word or phrase more than once, and it can be used for several

    purposes in poetry. How is repetition used in "Sssshhhhhhh"? _____

    _____

    _____

    _____

21. When a reader takes clues from literature and uses them to come to a conclusion about

    meaning, the reader is making an **inference**. Using the title of "Quiet Decision," the

    description of Hà's cutting of the sweet potato, and the dialogue at the end of the

    poem, what inference can be made about Mother's thinking? _____

    _____

    _____

22. A **metaphor** is a comparison between two things that does not use like or as. Identify

    one simile and one metaphor from "Crisscrossed Packs." _____

    _____

    _____

    _____

23. In addition to necessities, each family member packs one "choice" item in their bag

    before leaving Vietnam. What does Hà choose to take? Why does she take it?

    _____

    _____

    _____

24. What happens to Hà's papaya tree before the family leaves Vietnam?

    _____

25. What are conditions like on the ship? _____

    _____

    _____

    _____

26. When the helicopter pilot comes aboard the ship, what news does he bring? _____

    _____

READING COMPREHENSION AND ANALYSIS QUESTIONS

Part II: AT SEA

1. Describe some of the challenges Hà and her family face on the ship as they flee Vietnam.

   _____

   _____

   _____

2. When Hà eats her ration of rice, what does she imagine? Why might she connect these two things "although one has nothing / to do with the other"? _____

   _____

   _____

   _____

3. After one week on the ship, what does Mother have Hà's older brother do for the children onboard? _____

   _____

4. What is Khôi's secret? _____

   _____

5. What does Hà give up in order to make Khôi feel better? _____

   _____

   _____

6. What do the doll and the chick **symbolize** for Hà and Khôi? Why is it important, then, that they throw these items overboard? _____

   _____

   _____

   _____

7. **Personification** means that human characteristics are given to objects. In "A Kiss", two objects are personified and their kiss begins a party. What objects are personified as kissing and why is their kiss cause for celebration? _____

_____

_____

_____

8. What does Hà notice about the soldier who helps her board the small boat to go to shore? Why does it stand out to her? _____

_____

_____

_____

9. Where does Hà's family land to wait in a camp? _____

10. What is nước mắm and how does it help the people in the camp? _____

_____

_____

11. What does the amethyst ring **symbolize**? _____

_____

12. What three countries are options for Hà's family's relocation? _____

_____

13. What do people need in order to leave the camp in Florida? What does Mother do to improve the family's chances of leaving? _____

_____

_____

14. Where does Hà's family go when they get a sponsor? _____

15. Describe the physical appearance of Hà's family's sponsor. _____

_____

_____

_____

READING COMPREHENSION AND ANALYSIS QUESTIONS

Part III: ALABAMA

1. Why does Hà's family repack their bags after arriving in Alabama? _____
   _____

2. What does Mother say is the most important priority for the children now that the
   family is in America? _____
   _____

3. What does "the cowboy" bring to Hà's family to eat? What do they think of the meal?
   _____
   _____
   _____

4. Describe Hà's family's new house and furniture. _____
   _____
   _____
   _____

5. What are the rules Hà discusses in "First Rule," "Second Rule," and "Third Rule"? Why
   does she find them frustrating? _____
   _____
   _____
   _____

6. Explain the title of "Neigh Not Hee." _____
   _____
   _____
   _____
   _____
   _____

7. Why does Miss Scott laugh sadly at Hà on her first day at school? _____

_____

_____

8. In "Rainbow," what two physical traits does Hà notice about the other students? What does she notice about herself in comparison to them? _____

_____

_____

_____

9. Based on Hà's description of her first school lunch, what food did she receive in the cafeteria? _____

10. What part of the school day does "Loud Outside" describe? What happens to Hà during this time? _____

_____

_____

11. How is Vũ treated by others at school? How is his response different from Hà's?

_____

_____

_____

_____

12. How will brother Khôi help Hà? _____

_____

_____

13. What happens in class to make Hà feel dumb? _____

_____

_____

14. What does Vũ ask to be called now? Why do you think he takes this name? _____

_____

_____

_____

15. Identify two **similes** at the beginning of "Neighbors." What do these similes reveal has happened to Hà's home? _____

_____

_____

_____

16. Who is the only neighbor who is welcoming to the family? What does she offer to do for them? _____

_____

_____

17. Why does Hà feel regret when she starts to learn English? _____

_____

_____

_____

18. In "HA LE LU DA" what do Hà and each of her family members do at church? What does Hà realize at the end of the poem? _____

_____

_____

_____

19. **Imagery** is descriptive language that uses one or more of the five senses: sight, sound, smell, touch, taste. Find examples of imagery from each of the five senses in "Can't Help."

SENSE	EXAMPLES
Sight	
Sound	"day of shouts and HA LE LU DAs"
Smell	
Touch	
Taste	

20. Why is October 14 Hà's "Most Relieved Day"? _____

_____

_____

_____

_____

_____

21. What does Hà do that makes her feel "Smart Again"? _____

_____

_____

22. What does Miss Scott teach Hà's class about Vietnam? What does she miss in her

lesson? _____

_____

_____

_____

23. What name does Pink Boy call Hà? Why is it offensive? _____

_____

_____

24. What experience has she had and what does Mrs. Washington know about Vietnam,

both the good and the bad?

_____

_____

_____

_____

25. Why do the children chant "Boo-Da" at Hà? _____

_____

_____

_____

26. What "Confessions" does Hà make to her mother? What does Hà believe her behavior

has caused? _____

_____

_____

_____

_____

27. How does Hà finally escape the bullying of Pink Boy? Why do people start to treat her better at school? _____

_____

_____

28. What are the "three packages of something orange and dried" that Mrs. Washington gives Hà for Christmas? _____

29. What does Hà do with the present? What does Mother do with the gift? What lesson does Hà learn from the gift? How can this lesson apply to her new life in Alabama?

_____

_____

_____

_____

_____

_____

_____

READING COMPREHENSION AND ANALYSIS QUESTIONS

Part IV: NOW ON

1. What gift does "Pem" (Pam) give Hà? _____
   _____

2. Why is Hà embarrassed by what she wears to school on the first day back from
   Christmas break? _____
   _____

3. What type of ceremony does Hà's family hold? What sign leads Mother to decide to
   have the ceremony? _____
   _____
   _____
   _____

4. What career does each of Hà's brothers want to have? _____
   _____
   _____
   _____
   _____

5. What is Mother's prediction for the family for the year 1976?_____
   _____
   _____
   _____
   _____

COMPREHENSION CHECK

Part I: Saigon

1. _____ The story takes place during
   a. World War II.
   b. the Korean War.
   c. the 1970s.
   d. the 1990s.

2. _____ The narrator of the story is
   a. Hà, a ten-year-old girl.
   b. Hà, a ten-year-old boy.
   c. Khôi, a fourteen-year-old girl.
   d. Khôi, a fourteen-year-old boy.

3. _____ At the beginning of the novel, the characters celebrate
   a. Christmas.
   b. Tết.
   c. Kwanzaa.
   d. Independence Day.

4. _____ What does Hà do with the money her mother gives her to spend at the market?
   a. She uses it as her mother instructed to buy supplies for the family.
   b. She uses it to buy supplies, but keeps a little of the money for herself to pay for school tuition.
   c. She uses it to buy supplies, but keeps a little of the money for herself to buy cookies and treats.
   d. She wastes the money on supplies for a birthday party.

5. _____ Hà's favorite food is
   a. rice.
   b. beans.
   c. papaya.
   d. grapes.

6. _____ How does life change for Hà's family as the soldiers from the Communist North approach Saigon?
   a. Her brother Quang talks more about joining the North as a soldier, and Mother worries.
   b. Children show up to Hà's school as refugees from the North, and she is barely able to find a seat at school.
   c. American soldiers arrive with crates of food, medicine, and even candy for the children.
   d. Prices for gas and food climb higher, and the sound of bombs comes closer.

7. _____ Where is Hà's father?
   a. captured during a navy mission; no one knows where he is
   b. in the North checking on Mother's family
   c. in the United States training for the navy
   d. in Guam at a refugee camp

8. _____ Which of Hà's brothers idolizes Bruce Lee and believes that the family should leave Vietnam to escape the war?
   a. Vũ
   b. Khôi
   c. Quang
   d. Sơn

9. _____ How will Hà's family escape Vietnam?
   a. on foot
   b. by boat
   c. by helicopter
   d. by airplane

10. _____ What one personal item does Hà take with her as the family leaves Vietnam?
    a. a baby chick
    b. family photos of her father and mother
    c. papaya seeds from her tree
    d. a doll with mouse bites on its face

COMPREHENSION CHECK

Part II: AT SEA

1. _____ While eating her ration of rice on the ship, Hà imagines
   a. Tết celebrations.
   b. her old school.
   c. papaya.
   d. sweet cookies.

2. _____ How does Hà's older brother help the children on the ship?
   a. He teaches English lessons.
   b. He teaches them how to fish.
   c. He shares his rations of rice with them.
   d. He teaches them how to sew.

3. _____ What does Hà take from the soldier who helps her board the small boat to travel to shore?
   a. He gives her a papaya.
   b. She plucks one of his arm hairs.
   c. He gives her a new doll.
   d. She steals a small packet of cookies from his pocket.

4. _____ The *first* camp Hà's family stays in is located in
   a. France.
   b. Florida.
   c. Guam.
   d. Canada.

5. _____ The *second* camp Hà's family stays in is located in
   a. France.
   b. Florida.
   c. Guam.
   d. Canada.

6. _____ What does Hà's mother do to improve the family's chances of getting a sponsor in the United States?
   a. She says that the family is willing to split up and go to different parts of the country.
   b. She goes to chef school and learns to cook very well so that a sponsor may want to hire her.
   c. She sells her amethyst ring so that she can pay a sponsor.
   d. She changes the family sponsor application to say that the family is Christian.

7. _____ The sponsor for Hà's family is
   a. a chubby man who wears a cowboy hat.
   b. a tall, thin lawyer who drives a red sports car.
   c. an older woman who lost her son in the Vietnam war.
   d. a young, single woman who wears a cross on her necklace.

PArT III: ALABAMA

1. _____ Why does Hà's family repack their bags soon after they unpack them in Alabama?
    a. Their sponsor's wife does not want them in the house.
    b. They want to return to the camp in Florida.
    c. They do not like their sponsor's wife.
    d. They have decided to go back to Vietnam.

2. _____ What does Mother say is the most important priority for the children now that the family is in America?
    a. remembering Vietnam
    b. making friends
    c. getting jobs
    d. learning English

3. _____ Hà's sponsor doesn't understand her when she asks if she can use his
    a. house.
    b. horse.
    c. hat.
    d. hotel.

4. _____ How do the other children treat Hà on her first day at school?
    a. They are very curious, asking several questions about Vietnam and her trip to the United States.
    b. They do not seem to notice her at all, and no one speaks to her.
    c. They welcome her to the class, and one girl suggests that she try out for the lead role in an upcoming school play.
    d. One boy leads the other students in bullying her during recess. He pulls her arm hair and pokes her.

5. _____ How does Mrs. Washington help Hà?
   a. She buys new clothes for Hà.
   b. She drives Hà to school.
   c. She tutors Hà in English.
   d. She helps Hà care for the papaya tree.

6. _____ After Mrs. Washington speaks to Hà's teacher, where is Hà able to eat lunch?
   a. in the cafeteria
   b. in the classroom
   c. in the bathroom
   d. at Mrs. Washington's house

7. _____ Who are the friends Hà meets during lunch?
   a. Pam and Steven
   b. Pink Boy and Steven
   c. Penny and Pink Boy
   d. Pam and Pink Boy

8. _____ What do the children, led by Pink Boy, chant at Hà?
   a. "Vietnam"
   b. "Boo-Da"
   c. "Hum bug"
   d. "Pancakes"

9. _____ Why do the children stop bullying Hà?
   a. She fights Pink Boy and everyone is scared of her.
   b. She, Pam, and Steven lead the class in an anti-bullying workshop.
   c. Her brother, Vu Lee, starts taking her home from school every day on his motorcycle. Everyone thinks that Vu Lee is cool.
   d. Her mother, Mrs. Washington, and her teacher have a meeting and stop the bullying.

10. _____ What does Mrs. Washington give Hà for Christmas?
    a. a doll
    b. a coat
    c. flower seeds
    d. dried papaya

Part IV: NOW ON

1. _____ What gift does "Pem" (Pam) give Hà?
   a. a doll
   b. a coat
   c. flower seeds
   d. dried papaya

2. _____ What does Hà wear to school accidentally because she thinks it is a regular dress?
   a. choir robe
   b. bath robe
   c. nightgown
   d. bed sheet

3. _____ What type of ceremony does Hà's family hold at their house?
   a. blessing of the house
   b. farewell ceremony for her father
   c. Tết celebration
   d. wedding for Quang

4. _____ What are Hà's brothers' career goals?
   a. Quang will study to be a doctor. Vu Lee will become a mechanic. Khôi wants to become a teacher.
   b. Quang will study to be a teacher. Vu Lee will go to Atlanta to work in a hotel. Khôi wants to become a doctor.
   c. Quang will study to be a lawyer. Vu Lee will go become a movie star. Khôi wants to become a poet.
   d. Quang will study to be an engineer. Vu Lee will go to San Francisco to become a chef. Khôi wants to become a veterinarian.

5. _____ What does Hà's mother predict for the future of the family?
   a. They will return to Vietnam within the year.
   b. The old and new will mix together as they get used to their new lives in America.
   c. Father will return and they will be wealthy and happy in America.
   d. They will stay in America, but their old lives in Vietnam will continue to be more important to them than anything in the future.

ESSAY QUESTION

ANALYSIS: Theme

Essay prompt: Choose one of the following themes and explain how that theme is developed in the novel. Use the planning guide below to prepare your response. Write your essay on a separate sheet of paper.

Themes (Choose one):

- Challenges make people stronger.
- The support of family can help people through the most difficult circumstances.
- People must learn from their past and accept changes in their lives in order to be happy.

PLANNING GUIDE

Theme:

_____

_____

Specific examples from the novel where this theme is present:

1) _____

_____

2) _____

_____

3) _____

_____

Remember to include an introduction, body paragraphs, and a conclusion in your essay.

ESSAY QUESTION

ANALYSIS: SYMBOLISM

Essay prompt: Choose one of the following symbols and explain how that symbol is important in the novel. Use the planning guide below to prepare your response. Write your essay on a separate sheet of paper.

Symbols (Choose one):

- papaya
- amethyst ring
- the doll

PLANNING GUIDE

Symbol you chose: _____

When does the symbol appear in the novel? (Include specific examples.)

What does the symbol represent?

How does the symbol help the reader understand the purpose of the novel?

Remember to include an introduction, body paragraphs, and a conclusion in your essay.

Name _____

Persuasion

Essay prompt: When Hà moves to the United States, she struggles to fit in with her peers and learn English.

Some experts in education argue that the best way to learn a new language and culture is through immersion: joining the group like Hà does. With immersion, students take classes with peers in their age group and learn English on their own over time.

However, other experts suggest that students new to the United States who do not speak English benefit from programs where they spend the majority of their time learning English with other non-English speakers. In these programs, students would only enter regular classes after they have mastered English.

Should non-English speakers be required to enter a special, separate language learning programs or should they take standard classes with students their age, learning English as they go?

Remember to include an introduction, body paragraphs, and a conclusion in your essay.

Part I: saigon

1. 1975
2. Lunar new year; families eat sweets and rice cakes. They dress in new clothes and celebrate a birthday. Everyone acts happy because they believe that the first few days will predict the way the rest of the year will go.
3. Ten years old
4. He says their lives will "twist inside out." The family will face challenges and change. Answers may vary.
5. Fill in the following chart for the characters in Hà's family:

Character	Descriptive details
Hà (Kim Hà)	Ten years old; named for the Golden River; loves her papaya tree
Mother	Practical and firm with her children; creative and industrious in providing for the family's needs; chants and burns incense; secretary in a naval office
Quang	Twenty one years old; studying engineering
Vũ	Eighteen years old; idolizes Bruce Lee
Khôi	Fourteen years old; wants to stay in Vietnam, keeps hens eggs and tries to hatch chicks

6. The papaya tree represents Hà herself. Very young, growing, and full of potential and promise, the tree and Hà are both growing in an increasingly dangerous context.
7. Hà's best friend, TiTi, flees Vietnam with her family. Khôi says that they are a rich family leaving the country on a cruise ship.
8. He was captured during a navy mission when Hà was a baby. Mother chants and burns incense in hopes of his return. The children avoid repeating phrases their father used so that they will not make their mother sad.
9. She buys a little less for the family than her mother requested, and she spends the extra money on treats for herself: toasted coconut, fried dough, and cookies.
10. The description of the papayas says that they will be "soft as a yam."
11. Most of the words in italics are dialogue. Students should pay attention to the speaker of each italicized section.
12. The Communists are coming closer to Saigon. As they approach, prices go up and the sound of bombs comes closer.

13. She married Hà's father and moved south. Her father was waiting for a family member to have a baby. However, before the baby was born, the border between North and South was closed. People could not travel or send letters, so Mother lost touch with her family.

14. The President says "We know you have suffered. / I thank you, / your country thanks you." Hà's mother clicks her tongue and says that the President's tears are "Tears of an ugly fish." She does not think he is being sincere.

15. "Her brows / twist like laundry / being wrung dry." The simile illustrates Mother's worry about how to feed her children with so little.

16. Hà pinches Tram because she is jealous of the skinny, nervous, teacher's pet.

17. Even though the situation in Saigon is getting worse, Hà still clings to her home, her school, and her family. This poem is placed between "Closed too Soon" about the closing of Hà's school, and "Bridge to the Sea" about a ship that will take Hà and her family away from Vietnam. Hà, like the papayas, is clinging to what she knows. The lines also highlight the fact that Hà, a young girl, still green, is clinging to her mother and her childhood. She is a smart, promising girl whose experience is about to force her to grow up quickly.

18. He was Hà's father's best friend and he has found a way to bypass the checkpoint leading to the port in order to get on a ship and flee Vietnam.

19. Khôi and Quang both believe the family should stay in Vietnam. However Vũ's love of Bruce Lee, and Western culture, makes him want to go to the US.

20. The word "stares" is repeated three times. It shows that Hà's brother pauses dramatically, waits, and pressures her into a pinky promise with him no to leave Vietnam,

21. Mother decides to leave Vietnam because she wants to provide a better life for her children.

22. Metaphor: The needle is a worm. Simile: Mother is like bark.

23. She takes a mouse-bitten doll. She says she loves the doll more because of her scars. This comment foreshadows the scars Hà will gain as she grows through the challenge of her move to Alabama.

24. Brother Vũ cuts it down.

25. Hot and extremely crowded.

26. Saigon has fallen to the Communists.

Part II: AT SEA

1. They hide below deck without lights or cooking. Hà needs to drink and use the restroom, but everyone is encouraged to drink as little as possible. Her family has very little food, and others do not share with them.

2. She imagines the taste of papaya. Though rice doesn't actually taste like the papaya, it reminds her of her childhood, innocence, and the safety of home, which connects the two foods.

3. Quang teaches English lessons.

4. With him he carries a chick that has died and causes a foul smell.

5. She gives up her doll to toss it into the ocean with his chick.

6. The doll and chick represent bits of childhood innocence and remembrance of home in Vietnam. The children are forced to let go of doll, chick, innocence, and home as they suffer through the journey on the ship.

7. An American ship and Hà's ship come together in a kiss. Everyone begins to celebrate because they have been saved.
8. She notices the soldiers fuzzy, golden arm hair, and she plucks a strand of it. The hair is very different from her own.
9. Guam
10. It is fish sauce and people use it to flavor their food.
11. It symbolizes the love between Hà's mother and father.
12. France, Canada, and the United States.
13. A sponsor; Mother changes the family's application to say that they are Christians.
14. Alabama
15. He is tall and chubby with blonde hair. He wears cowboy hats and smokes cigars.

Part III: ALABAMA

1. The wife of their sponsor is not welcoming to them.
2. She insists that they must learn English.
3. He brings American fried chicken. They think the chicken is flavorless and disgusting.
4. The house has two bedrooms and perks like a washing machine, stove, and shower. However, Hà doesn't like the old, stained, donated furniture and dishes. The chairs and sofa are pink and green and the dishes don't match.
5. These are rules of English, specifically rules about adding "s" to words. She thinks there is a lot of hissing in English, and she is confused by the exceptions to the rules.
6. Hà thinks that her sponsor is a cowboy, and she tries to ask to ride his horse. She makes the sound for a horse: "hee, hee, hee." In America, people say that the sound of a horse is "Neigh Not Hee." Hà is having a difficult time understanding her now home.
7. Hà tries to tell Miss Scott her name. The teacher misunderstands and pities Hà, thinking that Hà is saying "ha," so she laughs sadly in response.
8. She notices their skin and hair. She is the only one with black hair and olive skin.
9. A hot dog.
10. The students go out for recess, and the children bully her. "Pink boy" leads the bullying by pulling her arm hair and poking her on the cheek and chest.
11. Someone calls him "Ching Chong" and trips him. Instead of running away from his bully like Hà did, he nearly kicks the boy in the face. He says he only wanted to scare the bully, not hurt him.
12. He will give her a ride to and from school on his bike.
13. Miss Scott makes the class clap for her when she says the alphabet, and the class claps when she counts to twenty.
14. He goes by the name Vu Lee, probably because it is similar to his hero, Bruce Lee.
15. "Eggs explode / like smears of snot" and "Bathroom paper hangs / like ghosts" are similes used to show that Hà's family has been harassed. Their house has been hit with eggs and their yard and trees covered with toilet paper.
16. Mrs. Washington, a retired teacher, offers to tutor Hà and her brothers.
17. The more words she knows, the more she understands the children who tease her, asking if she eats dog meat and if she lived in a jungle.

18. They are each dunked underwater, baptized, and they are kissed by each of the church members as they pass by. Hà gets chills as she realizes that the family will come back to the church every week.

19. Sight: "Mother taps her nails / on the dining table" / Sound: "Mother taps her nails / on the dining table", "quiet tones", "day of shouts and HA LE LU DAs", "Clang clang clang", "clear-stream bell echoes" / Smell: "Ashy bitter citrus", "floral wafts", "lavender scent", "traces of lavender" / Touch: "I shuffle off", "I lie frozen" / Taste: "tasting ripe papaya"

20. Hà tells Mrs. Washington that she hides in the bathroom during lunch. Mrs. Washington makes talks to Miss Scott and packs a lunch so that Hà can eat in the classroom instead of the lunchroom. Hà meets Pam and Steven during lunch.

21. Pink Boy cannot solve a math problem, but Hà goes to the board and finds the answer simply.

22. She share with them images of violence, war, and refugees. Hà wishes that she had shared something about the good times in Vietnam: papayas and Tết.

23. He calls her pancake face. He's making fun of the flatness of her face.

24. Mrs. Washington's son was killed in the war, but she has photos of the beauty and joy in the country. She lets Hà take home a book of pictures of school girls, papaya trees, and celebrations from Vietnam.

25. Miss Scott taught another lesson on Vietnam, showing a picture of Buddha. She invited Hà to speak and Hà said, "I know Buddha." The children, led by Pink Boy continue to bully her by chanting "Boo-Da."

26. Hà tells her mother that she used to buy treats for herself at market and pinch the girl next to her in school. Also, she reveals that she tapped her toe on the floor on Tết. She thinks that she is being punished for her bad behavior, and she believes she ruined the luck of her entire family.

27. Vu Lee arrives on his motorcycle to help Hà, and he picks her up from school every day. The other kids think her brother is cool, so they stop bullying Hà.

28. Dried papaya.

29. Hà throws away the papaya, but her mother soaks the fruit in water. When she eats the fruit, Hà decides that it is "Not the same, / but not bad / at all." Similarly, she has learned that her life in Alabama is different and she has had to face challenges, but it is not necessarily bad.

Part IV: NOW ON

1. A doll with long black hair.

2. She wears a flannel nightgown thinking that it is a regular dress.

3. The family holds a farewell ceremony for Hà's father. After losing the amethyst ring, Mother has realized that Hà's father will never return.

4. Quang will study to be an engineer. Vu Lee will go to San Francisco to become a chef. Khôi wants to become a veterinarian.

5. "Our lives / will twist and twist, / intermingling the old and the new / until it doesn't matter / which is which."

Part I: Saigon

1. C
2. A
3. B
4. C
5. C
6. D
7. A
8. A
9. B
10. D

Part II: AT SEA

1. C
2. A
3. B
4. C
5. B
6. D
7. A

Part III: ALABAMA

1. A
2. D
3. B
4. D
5. C
6. B
7. A
8. B
9. C
10. D

Part IV: ALABAMA

1. A
2. C
3. B
4. D
5. B

Student name: _____

	EXCELLENT	ACCEPTABLE	NEEDS IMPROVEMENT
SUPPORTING EXAMPLES Score: ____ / ____	*Essay provides at least three specific examples from the text clearly related to the theme.*	*Essay provides some examples, but the examples may not connect as clearly to the theme. The student may need an additional example.*	*Not enough examples provided OR examples provided do not relate to the theme.*
ANALYSIS OF THEME Score: ____ / ____	*Essay explains how the theme is developed in the novel. Student commentary is original and insightful.*	*Essay may connect examples to theme, but the connections are not as strong as those provided in top level essays.*	*Essay does not provide analysis of theme.*
ORGANIZATION Score: ____ / ____	*Essay is organized with clear introduction, body paragraphs, and conclusion. Each paragraph includes a topic sentence and concluding sentence.*	*Essay is organized overall, but may exhibit minor lapses in paragraph structure.*	*Key organizational structures - introduction, body paragraphs, topic sentences, conclusion - are missing.*
GRAMMAR AND MECHANICS Score: ____ / ____	*No errors in grammar or mechanics*	*Few errors in grammar and/or mechanics*	*Several errors in grammar and/or mechanics*

Grade: _____ / _____

Comments:

Student name: _____

	EXCELLENT	ACCEPTABLE	NEEDS IMPROVEMENT
SUPPORTING EXAMPLES Score: _____ / _____	*Essay provides at least three specific examples from the text clearly related to the symbol.*	*Essay provides some examples, but the examples may not connect as clearly to the symbol. The essay may need an additional example.*	*Not enough examples provided or examples provided do not relate to the symbol.*
ANALYSIS OF SYMBOL Score: _____ / _____	*Essay explains how the symbol is developed in the novel. Student commentary is original and insightful.*	*Essay may connect examples to symbol, but the connections are not as strong as those provided in top level essays.*	*Essay does not provide analysis of symbol.*
ORGANIZATION Score: _____ / _____	*Essay is organized with clear introduction, body paragraphs, and conclusion. Each paragraph includes a topic sentence and concluding sentence.*	*Essay is organized overall, but may exhibit minor lapses in paragraph structure.*	*Key organizational structures - introduction, body paragraphs, topic sentences, conclusion - are missing.*
GRAMMAR AND MECHANICS Score: _____ / _____	*No errors in grammar or mechanics*	*Few errors in grammar and/or mechanics*	*Several errors in grammar and/or mechanics*

Grade: _____ / _____

Comments:

Student name: _____

	EXCELLENT	ACCEPTABLE	NEEDS IMPROVEMENT
SUPPORT Score: ____ / ____	*Essay clearly supports thesis with examples in body paragraphs.*	*Thesis may be adequately supported, but examples and arguments are less convincing than top level essays.*	*Lack of adequate support.*
CLEAR ARGUMENT Score: ____ / ____	*Thesis clearly indicates one argument. Argument is consistent throughout the essay.*	*Thesis chooses one side, but focus may shift at times throughout the essay.*	*Thesis is unclear.*
ORGANIZATION Score: ____ / ____	*Essay is organized with clear introduction, body paragraphs, and conclusion. Each paragraph includes a topic sentence and concluding sentence.*	*Essay is organized overall, but may exhibit minor lapses in paragraph structure.*	*Key organizational structures - introduction, body paragraphs, topic sentences, conclusion - are missing.*
GRAMMAR AND MECHANICS Score: ____ / ____	*No errors in grammar or mechanics*	*Few errors in grammar and/or mechanics*	*Several errors in grammar and/or mechanics*

Grade: _____ / _____

Comments:

Made in the USA
San Bernardino, CA
13 May 2018